PENGUIN BOOKS — GREAT IDEAS

Reflections on the Guillotine

Albert Camus

1913–1960

Albert Camus

Reflections on the Guillotine

Translated by Justin O'Brien

PENGUIN BOOKS — GREAT IDEAS

PENGUIN BOOKS

UK | USA | Canada | Ireland | Australia
India | New Zealand | South Africa

Penguin Books is part of the Penguin Random House group
of companies whose addresses can be found at
global.penguinrandomhouse.com.

First published in *Réflexions sur la peine Capitale*, by Arthur Koestler
and Albert Camus, Calmann-Lévy 1957
Published in *Committed Writings*, Penguin Classics 2020
This edition published in Penguin Books 2020
003

Text copyright © Calmann-Lévy, 1957
Translation copyright © Alfred A. Knopf, Inc, 1960

Set in 12/15 pt Dante MT Std
Typeset by Jouve (UK), Milton Keynes
Printed and bound in Great Britain by Clays Ltd, Elcograf S.p.A.

A CIP catalogue record for this book
is available from the British Library

ISBN: 978–0–241–47522–5

www.greenpenguin.co.uk

Reflections on the Guillotine

Shortly before the war of 1914, an assassin whose crime was particularly repulsive (he had slaughtered a family of farmers, including the children) was condemned to death in Algiers. He was a farm worker who had killed in a sort of bloodthirsty frenzy but had aggravated his case by robbing his victims. The affair created a great stir. It was generally thought that decapitation was too mild a punishment for such a monster. This was the opinion, I have been told, of my father, who was especially aroused by the murder of the children. One of the few things I know about him, in any case, is that he wanted to witness the execution, for the first time in his life. He got up in the dark to go to the place of execution at the other end of town amid a great crowd of people. What he saw that morning he never told anyone. My mother relates merely that he came rushing home, his face distorted, refused to talk, lay down for a moment on the bed, and suddenly began to vomit. He had just discovered the reality hidden under the noble phrases with which it was masked. Instead of thinking of the slaughtered children, he could think of nothing but that quivering body that had just been dropped onto a board to have its head cut off.

Presumably that ritual act is horrible indeed if it manages to overcome the indignation of a simple, straightforward man and if a punishment he considered richly deserved had no other effect in the end than to nauseate him. When the extreme penalty simply causes vomiting on the part of the respectable citizen it is supposed to protect, how can anyone maintain that it is likely, as it ought to be, to bring more peace and order into the community? Rather, it is obviously no less repulsive than the crime, and this new murder, far from making amends for the harm done to the social body, adds a new blot to the first one. Indeed, no one dares speak directly of the ceremony. Officials and journalists who have to talk about it, as if they were aware of both its provocative and its shameful aspects, have made up a sort of ritual language, reduced to stereotyped phrases. Hence we read at breakfast time in a corner of the newspaper that the condemned 'has paid his debt to society' or that he has 'atoned' or that 'at five a.m. justice was done.' The officials call the condemned man 'the interested party' or 'the patient' or refer to him by a number. People write of capital punishment as if they were whispering. In our well-policed society we recognize that an illness is serious from the fact that we don't dare speak of it directly. For a long time, in middle-class families people said no more than that the elder daughter had a 'suspicious cough' or that the father had a 'growth' because tuberculosis and cancer were looked upon as somewhat shameful maladies. This is probably even truer of capital punishment since everyone strives to refer to it only through euphemisms. It is to the body politic what cancer is to the individual body, with this difference: no one has ever spoken of the necessity of cancer. There is no hesitation, on the other hand, about presenting capital punishment as a regrettable necessity, a necessity that justifies killing because it is necessary, and let's not talk about it because it is regrettable.

But it is my intention to talk about it crudely. Not because I like scandal, nor, I believe, because of an unhealthy streak in my nature. As a writer, I have always loathed avoiding the issue; as a man, I believe that the repulsive aspects of our condition, if they are inevitable, must merely be faced in silence. But when silence or tricks of language contribute to maintaining an abuse that must be reformed or a suffering that can be relieved, then there is no other solution but to speak out and show the obscenity hidden under the verbal cloak. France shares with England and Spain the honor of being one of the last countries this side of the iron curtain to keep capital punishment in its arsenal of repression. The survival of such a primitive rite has been made possible among us only by the thoughtlessness or ignorance of the public, which reacts only with the ceremonial phrases that have been drilled into it. When the imagination sleeps, words are emptied of their meaning: a deaf population absent-mindedly registers the condemnation of a man. But if people are shown the machine, made to touch the wood and steel and to hear the sound of a head falling, then public imagination, suddenly awakened, will repudiate both the vocabulary and the penalty.

When the Nazis in Poland indulged in public executions of hostages, to keep those hostages from shouting words of revolt and liberty they muzzled them with a plaster-coated gag. It would be shocking to compare the fate of those innocent victims with that of condemned criminals. But, aside from the fact that criminals are not the only ones to be guillotined in our country, the method is the same. We smother under padded words a penalty whose legitimacy we could assert only after we had examined the penalty in reality. Instead of saying that the death penalty is first of all necessary and then adding that it is better not to talk about it, it is essential to say what it really is and then say whether, being what it is, it is to be considered as necessary.

So far as I am concerned, I consider it not only useless but definitely harmful, and I must record my opinion here before getting to the subject itself. It would not be fair to imply that I reached this conclusion as a result of the weeks of investigation and research I have just devoted to this question. But it would be just as unfair to attribute my conviction to mere mawkishness. I am far from indulging in the flabby pity characteristic of humanitarians, in which values and responsibilities fuse, crimes are balanced against one another, and innocence finally loses its rights. Unlike many of my well-known contemporaries, I do not think that man is by nature a social animal. To tell the truth, I think just the reverse. But I believe, and this is quite different, that he cannot live henceforth outside of society, whose laws are necessary to his physical survival. Hence the responsibilities must be established by society itself according to a reasonable and workable scale. But the law's final justification is in the good it does or fails to do to the society of a given place and time. For years I have been unable to see anything in capital punishment but a penalty the imagination could not endure and a lazy disorder that my reason condemned. Yet I was ready to think that my imagination was influencing my judgment. But, to tell the truth, I found during my recent research nothing that did not strengthen my conviction, nothing that modified my arguments. On the contrary, to the arguments I already had others were added. Today I share absolutely Koestler's conviction: the death penalty besmirches our society, and its upholders cannot reasonably defend it. Without repeating his decisive defense, without piling up facts and figures that would only duplicate others (and Jean Bloch-Michel's make them useless), I shall merely state reasons to be added to

Koestler's; like his, they argue for an immediate abolition of the death penalty.

We all know that the great argument of those who defend capital punishment is the exemplary value of the punishment. Heads are cut off not only to punish but to intimidate, by a frightening example, any who might be tempted to imitate the guilty. Society is not taking revenge; it merely wants to forestall. It waves the head in the air so that potential murderers will see their fate and recoil from it.

This argument would be impressive if we were not obliged to note:

1. that society itself does not believe in the exemplary value it talks about;
2. that there is no proof that the death penalty ever made a single murderer recoil when he had made up his mind, whereas clearly it had no effect but one of fascination on thousands of criminals;
3. that, in other regards, it constitutes a repulsive example, the consequences of which cannot be foreseen.

To begin with, society does not believe in what it says. If it really believed what it says, it would exhibit the heads. Society would give executions the benefit of the publicity it generally uses for national bond issues or new brands of drinks. But we know that executions in our country, instead of taking place publicly, are now perpetrated in prison courtyards before a limited number of specialists. We are less likely to know why and since when. This is a relatively recent measure. The last public execution, which took place in 1939, beheaded Weidmann, the author of several murders, who was notorious for his crimes. That morning a large crowd gathered at Versailles, including a large number of photographers. Between the moment when Weidmann was shown to the crowd and the moment when he was decapitated, photographs could be taken. A few hours later *Paris-Soir* published a page of illustrations of that appetizing event. Thus the good people of Paris could see that the light precision instrument used by the executioner was as different from the historical scaffold as a Jaguar is from one of our old Pierce-Arrows. The administration and the government, contrary to all hope, took such excellent publicity very badly and protested that the press had tried to satisfy the sadistic instincts of its readers. Consequently, it was decided that executions would no longer take place publicly, an arrangement that, soon after, facilitated the work of the occupation authorities. Logic, in that affair, was not on the side of the lawmaker.

On the contrary, a special decoration should have been awarded to the editor of *Paris-Soir*, thereby encouraging him to do better the next time. If the penalty is intended to be exemplary, then, not only should the photographs be multiplied, but the machine should even be set on a platform in Place de la Concorde at two p.m., the entire population should be invited, and the ceremony should be put on television for those who couldn't attend. Either this must be done or else there must be no more talk of exemplary value. How can a furtive assassination committed at night in a prison courtyard be exemplary? At most, it serves the purpose of periodically informing the citizens that they will die if they happen to kill – a future that can be promised even to those who do not kill. For the penalty to be truly exemplary it must be frightening. Tuaut de La Bouverie, representative of the people in 1791 and a partisan of public executions, was more logical when he declared to the National Assembly: 'It takes a terrifying spectacle to hold the people in check.'

Today there is no spectacle, but only a penalty known to all by hearsay and, from time to time, the news of an execution dressed up in soothing phrases. How could a future criminal keep in mind, at the moment of his crime, a sanction that everyone strives to make more and more abstract? And if it is really desired that he constantly keep that sanction in mind so that it will first balance and later reverse a frenzied decision, should there not be an effort to engrave that sanction and its dreadful reality in the sensitivity of all by every visual and verbal means?

Instead of vaguely evoking a debt that someone this very morning paid society, would it not be a more effective example to remind each taxpayer in detail of what he may expect? Instead of saying: 'If you kill, you will atone for it on the scaffold,' wouldn't it be better to tell him, for purposes of example: 'If you kill, you will be imprisoned for months or years, torn between an impossible despair and a constantly renewed terror, until one morning we shall slip into your cell after removing our shoes the better to take you by surprise while you are sound asleep after the night's anguish. We shall fall on you, tie your hands behind your back, cut with scissors your shirt collar and your hair if need be. Perfectionists that we are, we shall bind your arms with a strap so that you are forced to stoop and your neck will be more accessible. Then we shall carry you, an assistant on each side supporting you by the arm, with your feet dragging behind through the corridors. Then, under a night sky, one of the executioners will finally seize you by the seat of your pants and throw you horizontally on a board while another will steady your head in the lunette and a third will let fall from a height of seven feet a hundred-and-twenty-pound blade that will slice off your head like a razor.'

For the example to be even better, for the terror to impress each of us sufficiently to outweigh at the right moment an irresistible desire for murder, it would be essential to go still further. Instead of boasting, with the pretentious thoughtlessness characteristic of us, of having invented this rapid and humane* method of killing condemned men, we should publish thousands of copies of the eyewitness accounts and medical reports describing the state of the body after the execution, to be read

---

* According to the optimistic Dr Guillotin, the condemned was not to feel anything. At most a 'slight sensation of coldness on his neck.'

in schools and universities. Particularly suitable for this purpose is the recent report to the Academy of Medicine made by Doctors Piedelièvre and Fournier. Those courageous doctors, invited in the interest of science to examine the bodies of the guillotined after the execution, considered it their duty to sum up their dreadful observations: 'If we may be permitted to give our opinion, such sights are frightfully painful. The blood flows from the blood vessels at the speed of the severed carotids, then it coagulates. The muscles contract and their fibrillation is stupefying; the intestines ripple and the heart moves irregularly, incompletely, fascinatingly. The mouth puckers at certain moments in a terrible pout. It is true that in that severed head the eyes are motionless with dilated pupils; fortunately they look at nothing and, if they are devoid of the cloudiness and opalescence of the corpse, they have no motion; their transparence belongs to life, but their fixity belongs to death. All this can last minutes, even hours, in sound specimens: death is not immediate . . . Thus, every vital element survives decapitation. The doctor is left with this impression of a horrible experience, of a murderous vivisection, followed by a premature burial.'

I doubt that there are many readers who can read that terrifying report without blanching. Consequently, its exemplary power and its capacity to intimidate can be counted on. There is no reason not to add to it eyewitness accounts that confirm the doctors' observations. Charlotte Corday's severed head blushed, it is said, under the executioner's slap. This will not shock anyone who listens to more recent observers. An executioner's assistant (hence hardly suspect of indulging in romanticizing and sentimentality) describes in these terms what he was forced to see: 'It was a madman undergoing a real attack of *delirium tremens* that we dropped under the blade. The head dies at once. But the body literally jumps about in the basket, straining on the cords. Twenty minutes later, at the cemetery, it is still quivering.' The present chaplain of the Santé prison, Father Devoyod (who does not seem opposed to capital punishment), gives in his book, *Les Délinquants*, an account that goes rather far and renews the story of Languille, whose decapitated head answered the call of his name: 'The morning of the execution, the condemned man was in a very bad mood and refused the consolations of religion. Knowing his heart of hearts and the affection he had for his wife, who was very devout, we said to him: "Come now, out of love for your wife, commune with yourself a moment before dying," and the condemned man accepted. He communed at length before the crucifix, then he seemed to pay no further attention to our presence. When he was executed, we were a short distance from him. His head fell into the trough in front of the guillotine and the body was immediately put into the basket; but, by some mistake, the basket was closed before the head was put in. The assistant who was carrying the head had to wait a moment until the basket was opened again; now, during that brief space of time we could see the condemned man's eyes fixed on me with a look of supplication, as if to ask forgiveness. Instinctively we made the sign of the cross to bless the head, and then the lids blinked, the expression of the eyes softened, and finally the look, that had remained full of expression, became vague . . .' The reader may or may not, according to his faith, accept the explanation provided by the priest. At least those eyes that 'had remained full of expression' need no interpretation.

I could adduce other first-hand accounts that would be just as hallucinating. But I, for one, could not go on. After all, I do not claim that capital punishment is exemplary, and the penalty seems to me just what it is, a crude surgery practiced under conditions that leave nothing edifying about it. Society, on the other hand, and the State, which is not so impressionable, can very well put up with such details and, since they extol an example, ought to try to get everyone to put up with them so that no one will be ignorant of them and the population, terrorized once and for all, will become Franciscan one and all. Whom do they hope to intimidate, otherwise, by that example forever hidden, by the threat of a punishment described as easy and swift and easier to bear, after all, than cancer, by a penalty submerged in the flowers of rhetoric? Certainly not those who are considered respectable (some of them are) because they are sleeping at that hour, and the great example has not been announced to them, and they will be eating their toast and marmalade at the time of the premature burial, and they will be informed of the work of justice, if perchance they read the newspapers, by an insipid news item that will melt like sugar in their memory. And, yet, those peaceful creatures are the ones who provide the largest percentage of homicides. Many such respectable people are potential criminals. According to a magistrate, the vast majority of murderers he had known did not know when shaving in the morning that they were going to kill later in the day. As an example and for the sake of security, it would be wiser, instead of hiding the execution, to hold up the severed head in front of all who are shaving in the morning.

Nothing of the sort happens. The State disguises executions and keeps silent about these statements and eyewitness accounts. Hence it doesn't believe in the exemplary value of the penalty, except by tradition and because it has never bothered to think about the matter. The criminal is killed because this has been done for centuries and, besides, he is killed in a way that was set at the end of the eighteenth century. Out of habit, people will turn to arguments that were used centuries ago, even though these arguments must be contradicted by measures that the evolution of public sensitivity has made inevitable. A law is applied without being thought out and the condemned die in the name of a theory in which the executioners do not believe. If they believed in it, this would be obvious to all. But publicity not only arouses sadistic instincts with incalculable repercussions eventually leading to another murder; it also runs the risk of provoking revolt and disgust in the public opinion. It would become harder to execute men one after another, as is done in our country today, if those executions were translated into vivid images in the popular imagination. The man who enjoys his coffee while reading that justice has been done would spit it out at the least detail. And the texts I have quoted might seem to vindicate certain professors of criminal law who, in their obvious inability to justify that anachronistic penalty, console themselves by declaring, with the sociologist Tarde, that it is better to cause death without causing suffering than it is to cause suffering without causing death. This is why we must approve the position of Gambetta, who, as an adversary of the death penalty, voted against a bill involving suppression of publicity for executions, declaring: 'If you suppress the horror of the spectacle, if you execute inside prisons, you will smother the public outburst of revolt that has taken place of late and you will strengthen the death penalty.'

Indeed, one must kill publicly or confess that one does not feel authorized to kill. If society justifies the death penalty by the necessity of the example, it must justify itself by making the publicity necessary. It must show the executioner's hands each time and force everyone to look at them – the over-delicate citizens and all those who had any responsibility in bringing the executioner into being. Otherwise, society admits that it kills without knowing what it is saying or doing. Or else it admits that such revolting ceremonies can only excite crime or completely upset opinion. Who could better state this than a magistrate at the end of his career, Judge Falco, whose brave confession deserves serious reflection: 'The only time in my life when I decided against a commutation of penalty and in favor of execution, I thought that, despite my position, I could attend the execution and remain utterly impassive. Moreover, the criminal was not very interesting: he had tormented his daughter and finally thrown her into a well. But, after his execution, for weeks and even months, my nights were haunted by that recollection . . . Like everyone else, I served in the war and saw an innocent generation die, but I can state that nothing gave me the sort of bad conscience I felt in the face of the kind of administrative murder that is called capital punishment.'

But, after all, why should society believe in that example when it does not stop crime, when its effects, if they exist, are invisible? To begin with, capital punishment could not intimidate the man who doesn't know that he is going to kill, who makes up his mind to it in a flash and commits his crime in a state of frenzy or obsession, nor the man who, going to an appointment to have it out with someone, takes along a weapon to frighten the faithless one or the opponent and uses it although he didn't want to or didn't think he wanted to. In other words, it could not intimidate the man who is hurled into crime as if into a calamity. This is tantamount to saying that it is powerless in the majority of cases. It is only fair to point out that in our country capital punishment is rarely applied in such cases. But the word 'rarely' itself makes one shudder.

Does it frighten at least that race of criminals on whom it claims to operate and who live off crime? Nothing is less certain. We can read in Koestler that at a time when pickpockets were executed in England, other pickpockets exercised their talents in the crowd surrounding the scaffold where their colleague was being hanged. Statistics drawn up at the beginning of the century in England show that out of 250 who were hanged, 170 had previously attended one or more executions.

And in 1886, out of 167 condemned men who had gone through the Bristol prison, 164 had witnessed at least one execution. Such statistics are no longer possible to gather in France because of the secrecy surrounding executions. But they give cause to think that around my father, the day of that execution, there must have been a rather large number of future criminals, who did not vomit. The power of intimidation reaches only the quiet individuals who are not drawn toward crime and has no effect on the hardened ones who need to be softened. In Koestler's essay and in the detailed studies will be found the most convincing facts and figures on this aspect of the subject.

It cannot be denied, however, that men fear death. The privation of life is indeed the supreme penalty and ought to excite in them a decisive fear. The fear of death, arising from the most obscure depths of the individual, ravages him; the instinct to live, when it is threatened, panics and struggles in agony. Therefore the legislator was right in thinking that his law was based upon one of the most mysterious and most powerful incentives of human nature. But law is always simpler than nature. When law ventures, in the hope of dominating, into the dark regions of consciousness, it has little chance of being able to simplify the complexity it wants to codify.

If fear of death is, indeed, a fact, another fact is that such fear, however great it may be, has never sufficed to quell human passions. Bacon is right in saying that there is no passion so weak that it cannot confront and overpower fear of death. Revenge, love, honor, pain, another fear manage to overcome it. How could cupidity, hatred, jealousy fail to do what love of a person or a country, what a passion for freedom manage to do? For centuries the death penalty, often accompanied by barbarous refinements, has been trying to hold crime in check; yet crime persists. Why? Because the instincts that are warring in man are not, as the law claims, constant forces in a state of equilibrium. They are variable forces constantly waxing and waning, and their repeated lapses from equilibrium nourish the life of the mind as electrical oscillations, when close enough, set up a current. Just imagine the series of oscillations, from desire to lack of appetite, from decision to renunciation, through which each of us passes in a single day, multiply these variations infinitely, and you will have an idea of psychological proliferation. Such lapses from equilibrium are generally too fleeting to allow a single force to dominate the whole being. But it may happen that one of the soul's forces breaks loose until it fills the whole field of consciousness; at such a moment no instinct, not even that of life, can oppose the tyranny of that irresistible force. For capital punishment to be really intimidating, human nature would have to be different; it would have to be as stable and serene as the law itself. But then human nature would be dead.

It is not dead. This is why, however surprising this may seem to anyone who has never observed or directly experienced human complexity, the murderer, most of the time, feels innocent when he kills. Every criminal acquits himself before he is judged. He considers himself, if not within his right, at least excused by circumstances. He does not think or foresee; when he thinks, it is to foresee that he will be forgiven altogether or in part. How could he fear what he considers highly improbable? He will fear death after the verdict but not before the crime. Hence the law, to be intimidating, should leave the murderer no chance, should be implacable in advance and particularly admit no extenuating circumstance. But who among us would dare ask this?

If anyone did, it would still be necessary to take into account another paradox of human nature. If the instinct to live is fundamental, it is no more so than another instinct of which the academic psychologists do not speak: the death instinct, which at certain moments calls for the destruction of oneself and of others. It is probable that the desire to kill often coincides with the desire to die or to annihilate oneself.* Thus, the instinct for self-preservation is matched, in variable proportions, by the instinct for destruction. The latter is the only way of explaining altogether the various perversions which, from alcoholism to drugs, lead an individual to his death while he knows full well what is happening. Man wants to live, but it is useless to hope that this desire will dictate all his actions. He also wants to be nothing; he wants the irreparable, and death for its own sake. So it happens that the criminal wants not only the crime but the suffering that goes with it, even (one might say, especially) if that suffering is exceptional. When that odd desire grows and becomes

---

* It is possible to read every week in the papers of criminals who originally hesitated between killing themselves and killing others.

dominant, the prospect of being put to death not only fails to stop the criminal, but probably even adds to the vertigo in which he swoons. Thus, in a way, he kills in order to die.

Such peculiarities suffice to explain why a penalty that seems calculated to frighten normal minds is in reality altogether unrelated to ordinary psychology. All statistics without exception, those concerning countries that have abolished execution as well as the others, show that there is no connection between the abolition of the death penalty and criminality.* Criminal statistics neither increase nor decrease. The guillotine exists, and so does crime; between the two there is no other apparent connection than that of the law. All we can conclude from the figures, set down at length in statistical tables, is this: for centuries crimes other than murder were punished with death, and the supreme punishment, repeated over and over again, did not do away with any

* Report of the English Select Committee of 1930 and of the English Royal Commission that recently resumed the study: 'All the statistics we have examined confirm the fact that abolition of the death penalty has not provoked an increase in the number of crimes.'

of those crimes. For centuries now, those crimes have no longer been punished with death. Yet they have not increased; in fact, some of them have decreased. Similarly, murder has been punished with execution for centuries and yet the race of Cain has not disappeared. Finally, in the thirty-three nations that have abolished the death penalty or no longer use it, the number of murders has not increased. Who could deduce from this that capital punishment is really intimidating?

Conservatives cannot deny these facts or these figures. Their only and final reply is significant. They explain the paradoxical attitude of a society that so carefully hides the executions it claims to be exemplary. 'Nothing proves, indeed,' say the conservatives, 'that the death penalty is exemplary; as a matter of fact, it is certain that thousands of murderers have not been intimidated by it. But there is no way of knowing those it has intimidated; consequently, nothing proves that it is not exemplary.' Thus, the greatest of punishments, the one that involves the last dishonor for the condemned and grants the supreme privilege to society, rests on nothing but an unverifiable possibility. Death, on the other hand, does not involve degrees or probabilities. It solidifies all things, culpability and the body, in a definitive rigidity. Yet it is administered among us in the name of chance and a calculation. Even if that calculation were reasonable, should there not be a certainty to authorize the most certain of deaths? However, the condemned is cut in two, not so much for the crime he committed but by virtue of all the crimes that might have been and were not committed, that can be and will not be committed. The most sweeping uncertainty in this case authorizes the most implacable certainty.

I am not the only one to be amazed by such a dangerous contradiction. Even the State condemns it, and such bad conscience explains in turn the contradiction of its own attitude. The State divests its executions of all publicity because it cannot assert, in the face of facts, that they ever served to intimidate criminals. The State cannot escape the dilemma Beccaria described when he wrote: 'If it is important to give the people proofs of power often, then executions must be frequent; but crimes will have to be frequent too, and this will prove that the death penalty does not make the complete impression that it should, whence it results that it is both useless and necessary.' What can the State do with a penalty that is useless and necessary, except to hide it without abolishing it?

The State will keep it then, a little out of the way, not without embarrassment, in the blind hope that one man at least, one day at least, will be stopped from his murderous gesture by thought of the punishment and, without anyone's ever knowing it, will justify a law that has neither reason nor experience in its favor. In order to continue claiming that the guillotine is exemplary, the State is consequently led to multiply very real murders in the hope of avoiding a possible murder which, as far as it knows or ever will know, may never be perpetrated. An odd law, to be sure, which knows the murder it commits and will never know the one it prevents.

What will be left of that power of example if it is proved that capital punishment has another power, and a very real one, which degrades men to the point of shame, madness, and murder?

It is already possible to follow the exemplary effects of such ceremonies on public opinion, the manifestations of sadism they arouse, the hideous vainglory they excite in certain criminals. No nobility in the vicinity of the gallows, but disgust, contempt, or the vilest indulgence of the senses. These effects are well known. Decency forced the guillotine to emigrate from Place de l'Hôtel de Ville to the city gates, then into the prisons. We are less informed as to the feelings of those whose job it is to attend such spectacles. Just listen then to the warden of an English prison who confesses to 'a keen sense of personal shame' and to the chaplain who speaks of 'horror, shame, and humiliation.' Just imagine the feelings of the man who kills under orders – I mean the executioner. What can we think of those officials who call the guillotine 'the shunting engine,' the condemned man 'the client' or 'the parcel'? The priest Bela Just, who accompanied more than thirty condemned men, writes: 'The slang of the administrators of justice is quite as cynical and vulgar as that of the criminals.' And here are the remarks of one of our assistant executioners on his journeys to the provinces: 'When we would start on a trip, it was always a lark, with taxis and the best restaurants part of the spree!' The same one says, boasting of the executioner's skill in releasing the blade: 'You could *allow yourself the fun* of pulling the client's hair.' The dissoluteness expressed here has other, deeper aspects. The clothing of the condemned belongs in principle to the executioner. The elder Deibler used to hang all such articles of clothing in a shed and *now and then would go and look at them*. But there are more serious aspects. Here is what our assistant executioner declares: 'The new executioner is batty about the guillotine. He sometimes spends days on end at home sitting on a chair, ready with hat and coat on, waiting for a summons from the Ministry.'

Yes, this is the man of whom Joseph de Maistre said that, for him to exist, there had to be a special decree from the divine power and that, without him, 'order yields to chaos, thrones collapse, and society disappears.' This is the man through whom society rids itself altogether of the guilty man, for the executioner signs the prison release and takes charge of a free man. The fine and solemn example, thought up by our legislators, at least produces one sure effect – to depreciate or to destroy all humanity and reason in those who take part in it directly. But, it will be said, these are exceptional creatures who find a vocation in such dishonor. They seem less exceptional when we learn that hundreds of persons offer to serve as executioners without pay. The men of our generation, who have lived through the history of recent years, will not be astonished by this bit of information. They know that behind the most peaceful and familiar faces slumbers the impulse to torture and murder. The punishment that aims to intimidate an unknown murderer certainly confers a vocation of killer on many another monster about whom there is no doubt. And since we are busy justifying our cruelest laws with probable considerations, let there be no doubt that out of those hundreds of men whose services were declined, one at least must have satisfied otherwise the bloodthirsty instincts the guillotine excited in him.

If, therefore, there is a desire to maintain the death penalty, let us at least be spared the hypocrisy of a justification by example. Let us be frank about that penalty which can have no publicity, that intimidation which works only on respectable people, so long as they are respectable, which fascinates those who have ceased to be respectable and debases or deranges those who take part in it. It is a penalty, to be sure, a frightful torture, both physical and moral, but it provides no sure example except a demoralizing one. It punishes, but it forestalls nothing; indeed, it may even arouse the impulse to murder. It hardly seems to exist, except for the man who suffers it – in his soul for months and years, in his body during the desperate and violent hour when he is cut in two without suppressing his life. Let us call it by the name which, for lack of any other nobility, will at least give the nobility of truth, and let us recognize it for what it is essentially: a revenge.

A punishment that penalizes without forestalling is indeed called revenge. It is a quasi-arithmetical reply made by society to whoever breaks its primordial law. That reply is as old as man; it is called the law of retaliation. Whoever has done me harm must suffer harm; whoever has put out my eye must lose an eye; and whoever has killed must die. This is an emotion, and a particularly violent one, not a principle. Retaliation is related to nature and instinct, not to law. Law, by definition, cannot obey the same rules as nature. If murder is in the nature of man, the law is not intended to imitate or reproduce that nature. It is intended to correct it. Now, retaliation does no more than ratify and confer the status of a law on a pure impulse of nature. We have all known that impulse, often to our shame, and we know its power, for it comes down to us from the primitive forests. In this regard, we French, who are properly indignant upon seeing the oil king in Saudi Arabia preach international democracy and call in a butcher to cut off a thief's hand with a cleaver, live also in a sort of Middle Ages without even the consolations of faith. We still define justice according to the rules of a crude arithmetic.* Can it be said at least that that arithmetic is exact and that justice, even when elementary, even when limited to legal revenge, is safeguarded by the death penalty? The answer must be no.

Let us leave aside the fact that the law of retaliation is inapplicable and that it would seem just as excessive to punish the incendiary by setting fire

* A few years ago I asked for the reprieve of six Tunisians who had been condemned to death for the murder, in a riot, of three French policemen. The circumstances in which the murder had taken place made difficult any division of responsibilities. A note from the executive office of the President of the Republic informed me that my appeal was being considered by the appropriate organization. Unfortunately, when that note was addressed to me I had already read two weeks earlier that the sentence had been carried out. Three of the condemned men had been put to death and the three others reprieved. The reasons for reprieving some rather than the others were not convincing. But probably it was essential to carry out three executions where there had been three victims.

to his house as it would be insufficient to punish
the thief by deducting from his bank account a
sum equal to his theft. Let us admit that it is just
and necessary to compensate for the murder of the
victim by the death of the murderer. But beheading is not simply death. It is just as different, in
essence, from the privation of life as a concentra-
tion camp is from prison. It is a murder, to be sure,
and one that arithmetically pays for the murder
committed. But it adds to death a rule, a public
premeditation known to the future victim, an
organization, in short, which is in itself a source of
moral sufferings more terrible than death. Hence
there is no equivalence. Many laws consider a premeditated crime more serious than a crime of
pure violence. But what then is capital punishment but the most premeditated of murders, to
which no criminal's deed, however calculated it
may be, can be compared? For there to be equivalence, the death penalty would have to punish a
criminal who had warned his victim of the date
at which he would inflict a horrible death on him
and who, from that moment onward, had con-
fined him at his mercy for months. Such a monster
is not encountered in private life.

There, too, when our official jurists talk of

putting to death without causing suffering, they don't know what they are talking about and, above all, they lack imagination. The devastating, degrading fear that is imposed on the condemned for months or years* is a punishment more terrible than death, and one that was not imposed on the victim. Even in the fright caused by the mortal violence being done to him, most of the time the victim is hastened to his death without knowing what is happening to him. The period of horror is counted out with his life, and hope of escaping the madness that has swept down upon that life probably never leaves him. On the other hand, the horror is parceled out to the man who is condemned to death. Torture through hope

* Roemen, condemned to death at the Liberation of France, remained seven hundred days in chains before being executed, and this is scandalous. Those condemned under common law, as a general rule, wait from three to six months for the morning of their death. And it is difficult, if one wants to maintain their chances of survival, to shorten that period. I can bear witness, moreover, to the fact that the examination of appeals for mercy is conducted in France with a seriousness that does not exclude the visible inclination to pardon, insofar as the law and customs permit.

alternates with the pangs of animal despair. The lawyer and chaplain, out of mere humanity, and the jailers, so that the condemned man will keep quiet, are unanimous in assuring him that he will be reprieved. He believes this with all his being and then he ceases to believe it. He hopes by day and despairs of it by night.* As the weeks pass, hope and despair increase and become equally unbearable. According to all accounts, the color of the skin changes, fear acting like an acid. 'Knowing that you are going to die is nothing,' said a condemned man in Fresnes. 'But not knowing whether or not you are going to live, that's terror and anguish.' Cartouche said of the supreme punishment: 'Why, it's just a few minutes that have to be lived through.' But it is a matter of months, not of minutes. Long in advance the condemned man knows that he is going to be killed and that the only thing that can save him is a reprieve, rather similar, for him, to the decrees of heaven. In any case, he cannot intervene, make a plea himself, or convince. Everything goes on outside of him. He

---

* Sunday not being a day of execution, Saturday night is always better in the cell blocks reserved for those condemned to death.

is no longer a man but a thing waiting to be handled by the executioners. He is kept as if he were inert matter, but he still has a consciousness which is his chief enemy.

When the officials whose job it is to kill that man call him a parcel, they know what they are saying. To be unable to do anything against the hand that moves you from one place to another, holds you or rejects you, is this not indeed being a parcel, or a thing, or, better, a hobbled animal? Even then an animal can refuse to eat. The condemned man cannot. He is given the benefit of a special diet (at Fresnes, Diet No. 4 with extra milk, wine, sugar, jam, butter); they see to it that he nourishes himself. If need be, he is forced to do so. The animal that is going to be killed must be in the best condition. The thing or the animal has a right only to those debased freedoms that are called whims. 'They are very touchy,' a top-sergeant at Fresnes says without the least irony of those condemned to death. Of course, but how else can they have contact with freedom and the dignity of the will that man cannot do without? Touchy or not, the moment the sentence has been pronounced the condemned man enters an imperturbable machine. For a certain number of weeks he travels along in the intricate machinery that determines his every gesture and eventually hands him over to those who will lay him down on the killing machine. The parcel is no longer subject to the laws of chance that hang over the living creature but to mechanical laws that allow him to foresee accurately the day of his beheading.

That day his being an object comes to an end. During the three quarters of an hour separating him from the end, the certainty of a powerless death stifles everything else; the animal, tied down and amenable, knows a hell that makes the hell he is threatened with seem ridiculous. The Greeks, after all, were more humane with their hemlock. They left their condemned a relative freedom, the possibility of putting off or hastening the hour of his death. They gave him a choice between suicide and execution. On the other hand, in order to be doubly sure, we deal with the culprit ourselves. But there could not really be any justice unless the condemned, after making known his decision months in advance, had approached his victim, bound him firmly, informed him that he would be put to death in an hour, and had finally used that hour to set up the apparatus of death. What criminal ever reduced his victim to such a desperate and powerless condition?

This doubtless explains the odd submissiveness that is customary in the condemned at the moment of their execution. These men who have nothing more to lose could play their last card, choose to die of a chance bullet or be guillotined in the kind of frantic struggle that dulls all the faculties. In a way, this would amount to dying freely. And yet, with but few exceptions, the rule is for the condemned to walk toward death passively in a sort of dreary despondency. That is probably what our journalists mean when they say that the condemned died courageously. We must read between the lines that the condemned made no noise, accepted his status as a parcel, and that everyone is grateful to him for this. In such a degrading business, the interested party shows a praiseworthy sense of propriety by keeping the degradation from lasting too long. But the compliments and the certificates of courage belong to the general mystification surrounding the death penalty. For the condemned will often be seemly in proportion to the fear he feels. He will deserve the praise of the press only if his fear or his feeling of isolation is great enough to sterilize him completely. Let there be no misunderstanding. Some among the condemned, whether political or not, die heroically, and they must be granted the proper admiration and respect. But the majority of them know only the silence of fear, only the impassivity of fright, and it seems to me that such terrified silence deserves even greater respect. When the priest Bela Just offers to write to the family of a young condemned man a few moments before he is hanged and hears the reply: 'I have no courage, even for that,' how can a priest, hearing that confession of weakness, fail to honor the most wretched and most sacred thing in man? Those who say nothing but leave a little pool on the spot from which they are taken – who would dare say they died as cowards? And how can we describe the men who reduced them to such cowardice? After all, every murderer when he kills runs the risk of the most dreadful of deaths, whereas those who kill him risk nothing except advancement.

No, what man experiences at such times is beyond all morality. Not virtue, nor courage, nor intelligence, nor even innocence has anything to do with it. Society is suddenly reduced to a state of primitive terrors where nothing can be judged. All equity and all dignity have disappeared. 'The conviction of innocence does not immunize against brutal treatment . . . I have seen authentic bandits die courageously whereas innocent men went to their deaths trembling in every muscle.' When the same man adds that, according to his experience, intellectuals show more weakness, he is not implying that such men have less courage than others but merely that they have more imagination. Having to face an inevitable death, any man, whatever his convictions, is torn asunder from head to toe.* The feeling of powerlessness and solitude of the condemned man, bound and up against the public coalition that demands his death, is in itself an unimaginable punishment. From this point of view, too, it would be better for the execution to be public. The actor in every man could then come to the aid of the terrified animal and help him cut a figure, even in his own eyes. But darkness and secrecy offer no recourse. In such a disaster, courage, strength of soul, even faith may be disadvantages. As a general rule, a man is undone by waiting for capital punishment well before he dies. Two deaths are inflicted on him, the first being worse than the

---

* A great surgeon, a Catholic himself, told me that as a result of his experience he did not even inform believers when they had an incurable cancer. According to him, the shock might destroy even their faith.

second, whereas he killed but once. Compared to such torture, the penalty of retaliation seems like a civilized law. It never claimed that the man who gouged out one of his brother's eyes should be totally blinded.

Such a basic injustice has repercussions, besides, on the relatives of the executed man. The victim has his family, whose sufferings are generally very great and who, most often, want to be avenged. They are, but the relatives of the condemned man then discover an excess of suffering that punishes them beyond all justice. A mother's or a father's long months of waiting, the visiting-room, the artificial conversations filling up the brief moments spent with the condemned man, the visions of the execution are all tortures that were not imposed on the relatives of the victim. Whatever may be the feelings of the latter, they cannot want the revenge to extend so far beyond the crime and to torture people who share their own grief. 'I have been reprieved, Father,' writes a condemned man, 'I can't yet realize the good fortune that has come my way. My reprieve was signed on April 30 and I was told Wednesday as I came back from the visiting-room. I immediately informed Papa and Mama, who had not yet left the prison. You can imagine their happiness.'* We can indeed imagine it, but only insofar as we can imagine their uninterrupted suffering until the moment of the reprieve, and the final despair of those who receive the other notification, which punishes, in iniquity, their innocence and their misfortune.

To cut short this question of the law of retaliation, we must note that even in its primitive form it can operate only between two individuals of whom one is absolutely innocent and the other absolutely guilty. The victim, to be sure, is innocent. But can the society that is supposed to represent the victim lay claim to innocence? Is it not responsible, at least in part, for the crime it punishes so severely? This theme has often been developed, and I shall not repeat the arguments that all sorts of thinkers have brought forth since the eighteenth century. They can be summed up anyway by saying that every society has the criminals it deserves. But

* Father Devoyod: op. cit. Equally impossible to read calmly the petitions for reprieve presented by a father or a mother who obviously does not understand such sudden misfortune.

insofar as France is concerned, it is impossible not to point out the circumstances that ought to make our legislators more modest. Answering an inquiry of the *Figaro* in 1952 on the death penalty, a colonel asserted that establishing hard labor for life as the most severe penalty would amount to setting up schools of crime. That high-ranking officer seemed to be ignorant, and I can only congratulate him, of the fact that we already have our schools of crime, which differ from our federal prisons in this notable regard: it is possible to leave them at any hour of the day or night; they are the taverns and slums, the glory of our Republic. On this point it is impossible to express oneself moderately.

Statistics show 64,000 overcrowded dwellings (from three to five persons per room) in the city of Paris alone. To be sure, the killer of children is a particularly vile creature who scarcely arouses pity. It is probable, too (I say probable), that none of my readers, forced to live in the same conditions, would go so far as to kill children. Hence there is no question of reducing the culpability of certain monsters. But those monsters, in decent dwellings, would perhaps have had no occasion to go so far. The least that can be said is that they are not alone guilty, and it seems strange that the right to punish them should be granted to the very people who subsidize, not housing, but the growing of beets for the production of alcohol.*

But alcohol makes this scandal even more shocking. It is known that the French nation is systematically intoxicated by its parliamentary majority, for generally vile reasons. Now, the proportion of alcohol's responsibility in the cause of bloodthirsty crimes is shocking. A lawyer (Maître Guillon) estimated it at 60 per cent. For Dr Lagriffe the proportion extends from 41.7 to 72 per cent. An investigation carried out in 1951 in the clearing-center of the Fresnes prison, among the common-law criminals, showed 29 per cent to be chronic alcoholics and 24 per cent to have an alcoholic inheritance. Finally, 95 per cent of the killers of children are alcoholics. These are impressive figures. We can balance them with an even more magnificent figure: the tax report of a firm producing *apéritifs*, which in 1953 showed a profit of 410 million francs. Comparison of these figures justifies informing the stockholders of that

* France ranks first among countries for its consumption of alcohol and fifteenth in building.

firm and the Deputies with a financial interest in alcohol that they have certainly killed more children than they think. As an opponent of capital punishment, I am far from asking that they be condemned to death. But, to begin with, it strikes me as indispensable and urgent to take them under military escort to the next execution of a murderer of children and to hand them on their way out a statistical report including the figures I have given.

The State that sows alcohol cannot be surprised to reap crime.* Instead of showing surprise, it simply goes on cutting off heads into which it has poured so much alcohol. It metes out justice imperturbably and poses as a creditor: its good conscience does not suffer at all. Witness the alcohol salesman who, in answer to the *Figaro's* inquiry, exclaimed: 'I know just what the staunchest enemy of the death penalty would do if, having

---

* The partisans of the death penalty made considerable publicity at the end of the last century about an increase in criminality beginning in 1880, which seemed to parallel a decrease in application of the penalty. But in 1880 a law was promulgated that permitted bars to be opened without any prior authorization. After that, just try to interpret statistics!

a weapon within reach, he suddenly saw assassins on the point of killing his father, his mother, his children, or his best friend. Well!' That 'well' in itself seems somewhat alcoholized. Naturally, the staunchest enemy of capital punishment would shoot those murderers, and rightly so, without thereby losing any of his reasons for staunchly defending abolition of the death penalty. But if he were to follow through his thinking and the afore-mentioned assassins reeked of alcohol, he would then go and take care of those whose vocation is to intoxicate future criminals. It is even quite surprising that the relatives of victims of alco-holic crimes have never thought of getting some enlightenment from the Parliament. Yet nothing of the sort takes place, and the State, enjoying gen-eral confidence, even supported by public opinion, goes on chastising assassins (particularly the alco-holics) somewhat in the way the pimp chastises the hard-working creatures who assure his livelihood. But the pimp at least does no moralizing. The State does. Although jurisprudence admits that drunkenness sometimes constitutes an extenuat-ing circumstance, the State is ignorant of chronic alcoholism. Drunkenness, however, accompanies only crimes of violence, which are not punished with death, whereas the chronic alcoholic is capable also of premeditated crimes, which will bring about his death. Consequently, the State reserves the right to punish in the only case in which it has a real responsibility.

Does this amount to saying that every alcoholic must be declared irresponsible by a State that will beat its breast until the nation drinks nothing but fruit juice? Certainly not. No more than that the reasons based on heredity should cancel all culpability. The real responsibility of an offender cannot be precisely measured. We know that arithmetic is incapable of adding up the number of our antecedents, whether alcoholic or not. Going back to the beginning of time, the figure would be twenty-two times, raised to the tenth power, greater than the number of present inhabitants of the earth. The number of bad or morbid predispositions our antecedents have been able to transmit to us is, thus, incalculable. We come into the world laden with the weight of an infinite necessity. One would have to grant us, therefore, a general irresponsibility. Logic would demand that neither punishment nor reward should ever be meted out, and, by the same token, all society would become impossible. The instinct of preservation of societies, and hence of individuals, requires instead that individual responsibility be postulated and accepted without dreaming of an absolute indulgence that would amount to the death of all society. But the same reasoning must lead us to conclude that there never exists any total responsibility or, consequently, any absolute punishment or reward. No one can be rewarded completely, not even the winners of Nobel Prizes. But no one should be punished absolutely if he is thought guilty, and certainly not if there is a chance of his being innocent. The death penalty, which really neither provides an example nor assures distributive justice, simply usurps an exorbitant privilege by claiming to punish an always relative culpability by a definitive and irreparable punishment.

If indeed capital punishment represents a doubtful example and an unsatisfactory justice, we must agree with its defenders that it is eliminative. The death penalty definitively eliminates the condemned man. That alone, to tell the truth, ought to exclude, for its partisans especially, the repetition of risky arguments which, as we have just seen, can always be contested. Instead, one might frankly say that it is definitive because it must be, and affirm that certain men are irremediable in society, that they constitute a permanent danger for every citizen and for the social order, and that therefore, before anything else, they must be suppressed. No one, in any case, can refute the existence in society of certain wild animals whose energy and brutality nothing seems capable of breaking. The death penalty, to be sure, does not solve the problem they create. Let us agree, at least, that it suppresses the problem.

I shall come back to such men. But is capital punishment applied only to them? Is there any assurance that none of those executed is remediable? Can it even be asserted that none of them is innocent? In both cases, must it not be admitted that capital punishment is eliminative only insofar as it is irreparable? The 15th of March, 1957, Burton Abbott was executed in California, condemned to death for having murdered a little girl of fourteen. Men who commit such a heinous crime are, I believe, classified among the irremediable. Although Abbott continually protested his innocence, he was condemned. His execution had been set for the 15th of March at ten o'clock. At 9:10 a delay was granted to allow his attorneys to make a final appeal.* At eleven o'clock the appeal was refused. At 11:15 Abbott entered the gas chamber. At 11:18 he breathed in the first whiffs of gas. At 11:20 the secretary of the Committee on Reprieves called on the telephone. The Committee had changed its mind. They had tried to reach the Governor, who was out sailing; then they had phoned the prison directly. Abbott was taken from the gas chamber. It was too late. If only it had been cloudy over California that day, the Governor would not have gone out sailing. He would have telephoned two minutes earlier; today Abbott would be alive and would perhaps see his innocence proved. Any other penalty, even the harshest, would have left him that chance. The death penalty left him none.

This case is exceptional, some will say. Our lives are exceptional, too, and yet, in the fleeting existence that is ours, this takes place near us, at some ten hours' distance by air. Abbott's misfortune is less an exception than a news item like so many others, a mistake that is not isolated if we can believe our newspapers (see the Deshays

* It must be noted that the custom in American prisons is to move the condemned man into another cell on the eve of his execution while announcing to him the ceremony in store for him.

case, to cite but the most recent one). The jurist Olivecroix, applying the law of probability to the chance of judicial error, around 1860, concluded that perhaps one innocent man was condemned in every two hundred and fifty-seven cases. The proportion is small? It is small in relation to average penalties. It is infinite in relation to capital punishment. When Hugo writes that to him the name of the guillotine is Lesurques,* he does not mean that all those who are decapitated are Lesurques, but that one Lesurques is enough for the guillotine to be permanently dishonored. It is understandable that Belgium gave up once and for all pronouncing the death penalty after a judicial error and that England raised the question of abolition after the Hayes case. It is also possible to understand the conclusions of the Attorney General who, when consulted as to the appeal of a very probably guilty criminal whose victim had not been found, wrote: 'The survival of X . . . gives the authorities the possibility of examining at leisure any new clue that might eventually be

---

* This is the name of the innocent man guillotined in the case of the *Courrier de Lyon*.

brought in as to the existence of his wife.* . . . On the other hand, the execution, by canceling that hypothetical possibility of examination, would, I fear, give to the slightest clue a theoretical value, a power of regret that I think it inopportune to create.' A love of justice and truth is expressed here in a most moving way, and it would be appropriate to quote often in our courts that 'power of regret' which so vividly sums up the danger that faces every juror. Once the innocent man is dead, no one can do anything for him, in fact, but to rehabilitate him, if there is still someone to ask for this. Then he is given back his innocence, which, to tell the truth, he had never lost. But the persecution of which he was a victim, his dreadful sufferings, his horrible death have been given him forever. It remains only to think of the innocent men of the future, so that these tortures may be spared them. This was done in Belgium. In France consciences are apparently untroubled.

Probably the French take comfort from the idea that justice has progressed hand in hand with

---

* The condemned man was accused of having killed his wife. But her body had not been found.

science. When the learned expert holds forth in court, it seems as if a priest has spoken, and the jury, raised in the religion of science, expresses its opinion. However, recent cases, chief among them the Besnard case, have shown us what a comedy of experts is like. Culpability is no better established for having been established in a test tube, even a graduated one. A second test tube will tell a different story, and the personal equation loses none of its importance in such dangerous mathematics. The proportion of learned men who are really experts is the same as that of judges who are psychologists, hardly any greater than that of serious and objective juries. Today, as yesterday, the chance of error remains. Tomorrow another expert testimony will declare the innocence of some Abbott or other. But Abbott will be dead, scientifically dead, and the science that claims to prove innocence as well as guilt has not yet reached the point of resuscitating those it kills.

Among the guilty themselves, is there any assurance that none but the irretrievable have been killed? All those who, like me, have at a period of their lives necessarily followed the assize courts know that a large element of chance enters into any sentence. The look of the accused, his antecedents (adultery is often looked upon as an aggravating circumstance by jurors who may or may not all have been always faithful), his manner (which is in his favor only if it is conventional – in other words, play-acting most of the time), his very elocution (the old hands know that one must neither stammer nor be too eloquent), the mishaps of the trial enjoyed in a sentimental key (and the truth, alas, is not always emotionally effective): so many flukes that influence the final decision of the jury. At the moment of the death verdict, one may be sure that to arrive at the most definite of penalties, an extraordinary combination of uncertainties was necessary. When it is known that the supreme verdict depends on the jury's evaluation of the extenuating circumstances, when it is known, above all, that the reform of 1832 gave our juries the power of granting *indeterminate* extenuating circumstances, it is possible to imagine the latitude left to the passing mood of the jurors. The law no longer foresees precisely the cases in which death is to be the outcome; so the jury decides after the event by guesswork. Inasmuch as there are never two comparable juries, the man who is executed might well not have been. Beyond reclaim in the eyes of the respectable people of Ille-et-Vilaine, he would have been granted a semblance of excuse by the good citizens of the Var. Unfortunately, the same blade falls in the two Départements. And it makes no distinction.

The temporal risks are added to the geographical risks to increase the general absurdity. The French Communist workman who has just been guillotined in Algeria for having put a bomb (discovered before it went off) in a factory locker room was condemned as much because of the general climate as because of what he did. In the present state of mind in Algeria, there was a desire at one and the same time to prove to the Arab opinion that the guillotine was designed for Frenchmen too and to satisfy the French opinion wrought up by the crimes of terrorism. At the same moment, however, the Minister who approved the execution was accepting Communist votes in his electoral district. If the circumstances had been different, the accused would have got off easy and his only risk, once he had become a Deputy of the party, would be finding himself having a drink at the same bar as the Minister someday. Such thoughts are bitter, and one would like them to remain alive in the minds of our leaders. They must know that times and customs change; a day comes when the guilty man, too rapidly executed, does not seem so black. But it is too late and there is no alternative but to repent or to forget. Of course, people forget. Nonetheless, society is no less affected. The unpunished crime, according to the Greeks, infected the whole city. But innocence condemned or crime too severely punished, in the long run, soils the city just as much. We know this, in France.

Such, it will be said, is human justice, and, despite its imperfections, it is better than arbitrariness. But that sad evaluation is bearable only in connection with ordinary penalties. It is scandalous in the face of verdicts of death. A classic treatise on French law, in order to excuse the death penalty for not involving degrees, states this: 'Human justice has not the slightest desire to assure such a proportion. Why? Because it knows it is frail.' Must we therefore conclude that such frailty authorizes us to pronounce an absolute judgment and that, uncertain of ever achieving pure justice, society must rush headlong, through the greatest risks, toward supreme injustice? If justice admits that it is frail, would it not be better for justice to be modest and to allow its judgments sufficient latitude so that a mistake can be corrected?* Could not justice concede to the criminal the same weakness in which society finds a sort of permanent extenuating circumstance for itself? Can the jury decently say: 'If I kill you by mistake, you will forgive me when you consider the weaknesses of our common nature. But I am condemning you to death without considering those weaknesses or that nature'? There is a solidarity of all men in error and aberration. Must that solidarity operate for the tribunal and be denied the accused? No, and if justice has any meaning in this world, it means nothing but the recognition of that solidarity; it cannot, by its very essence, divorce itself from compassion. Compassion, of course, can in this instance be but awareness of a common suffering and not a frivolous indulgence paying no attention to the sufferings and rights of the victim. Compassion does not exclude punishment, but it suspends the final condemnation. Compassion

---

* We congratulated ourselves on having reprieved Sillon, who recently killed his four-year-old daughter in order not to give her to her mother, who wanted a divorce. It was discovered, in fact, during his imprisonment that Sillon was suffering from a brain tumor that might explain the madness of his deed.

loathes the definitive, irreparable measure that does an injustice to mankind as a whole because of failing to take into account the wretchedness of the common condition.

To tell the truth, certain juries are well aware of this, for they often admit extenuating circumstances in a crime that nothing can extenuate. This is because the death penalty seems excessive to them in such cases and they prefer not punishing enough to punishing too much. The extreme severity of the penalty then favors crime instead of penalizing it. There is not a court session during which we do not read in the press that a verdict is incoherent and that, in view of the facts, it seems either insufficient or excessive. But the jurors are not ignorant of this. However, faced with the enormity of capital punishment, they prefer, as we too should prefer, to look like fools rather than to compromise their nights to come. Knowing themselves to be fallible, they at least draw the appropriate consequences. And true justice is on their side precisely insofar as logic is not.

There are, however, major criminals whom all juries would condemn at any time and in any place whatever. Their crimes are not open to doubt, and the evidence brought by the accusation is confirmed by the confessions of the defense. Most likely, everything that is abnormal and monstrous in them is enough to classify them as pathological. But the psychiatric experts, in the majority of cases, affirm their responsibility. Recently in Paris a young man, somewhat weak in character but kind and affectionate, devoted to his family, was, according to his own admission, annoyed by a remark his father made about his coming home late. The father was sitting reading at the dining-room table. The young man seized an ax and dealt his father several blows from behind. Then in the same way he struck down his mother, who was in the kitchen. He undressed, hid his bloodstained trousers in the closet, went to make a call on the family of his fiancée, without showing any signs, then returned home and notified the police that he had just found his parents murdered. The police immediately discovered the bloodstained trousers and, without difficulty, got a calm confession from the parricide. The psychiatrists decided that this man who murdered through annoyance was responsible. His odd indifference, of which he was to give other indications in prison (showing pleasure because his parents' funeral had attracted so many people – 'They were much loved,' he told his lawyer), cannot, however, be considered as normal. But his reasoning power was apparently untouched.

Many 'monsters' offer equally impenetrable exteriors. They are eliminated on the mere consideration of the facts. Apparently the nature or the magnitude of their crimes allows no room for imagining that they can ever repent or reform. They must merely be kept from doing it again, and there is no other solution but to eliminate them. On this frontier, and on it alone, discussion about the death penalty is legitimate. In all other cases the arguments for capital punishment do not stand up to the criticisms of the abolitionists. But in extreme cases, and in our state of ignorance, we make a wager. No fact, no reasoning can bring together those who think that a chance must always be left to the vilest of men and those who consider that chance illusory. But it is perhaps possible, on that final frontier, to go beyond the long opposition between partisans and adversaries of the death penalty by weighing the advisability of that penalty today, and in Europe. With much less competence, I shall try to reply to the wish expressed by a Swiss jurist, Professor Jean Graven, who wrote in 1952 in his remarkable study on the problem of the death penalty: 'Faced with the problem that is once more confronting our conscience and our reason, we think that a solution must be sought, not through the conceptions, problems, and arguments of the past, nor through the hopes and theoretical promises of the future, but through the ideas, recognized facts, and necessities of the present.' It is possible, indeed, to debate endlessly as to the benefits or harm attributable to the death penalty through the ages or in an intellectual vacuum. But it plays a role here and now, and we must take our stand here and now in relation to the modern executioner. What does the death penalty mean to the men of the mid-century?

To simplify matters, let us say that our civilization has lost the only values that, in a certain way, can justify that penalty and, on the other hand, suffers from evils that necessitate its suppression. In other words, the abolition of the death penalty ought to be asked for by all thinking members of our society, for reasons both of logic and of realism.

Of logic, to begin with. Deciding that a man must have the definitive punishment imposed on him is tantamount to deciding that that man has no chance of making amends. This is the point, to repeat ourselves, where the arguments clash blindly and crystallize in a sterile opposition. But it so happens that none among us can settle the question, for we are all both judges and interested parties. Whence our uncertainty as to our right to kill and our inability to convince each other. Without absolute innocence, there is no supreme judge. Now, we have all done wrong in our lives even if that wrong, without falling within the jurisdiction of the laws, went as far as the unknown crime. There are no just people – merely hearts more or less lacking in justice. Living at least allows us to discover this and to add to the sum of our actions a little of the good that will make up in part for the evil we have added to the world. Such a right to live, which allows a chance to make amends, is the natural right of every man, even the worst man. The lowest of criminals and the most upright of judges meet side by side, equally wretched in their solidarity. Without that right, moral life is utterly impossible. None among us is authorized to despair of a single man, except after his death, which transforms his life into destiny and then permits a definitive judgment. But pronouncing the definitive judgment before his death, decreeing the closing of accounts when the creditor is still alive, is no man's right. On this limit, at least, whoever judges absolutely condemns himself absolutely.

Bernard Fallot of the Masuy gang, working for the Gestapo, was condemned to death after admitting the many terrible crimes of which he was guilty, and declared himself that he could not be pardoned. 'My hands are too red with blood,' he told a prison mate. Public opinion and the opinion of his judges certainly classed him among the irremediable, and I should have been tempted to agree if I had not read a surprising testimony. This is what Fallot said to the same companion after declaring that he wanted to die courageously: 'Shall I tell you my greatest regret? Well, it is not having known the Bible I now have here. I assure you that I wouldn't be where I now am.' There is no question of giving in to some conventional set of sentimental pictures and calling to mind Victor Hugo's good convicts. The age of enlightenment, as people say, wanted to suppress the death penalty on the pretext that man was naturally good. Of course he is not (he is worse or better). After twenty years of our magnificent history we are well aware of this. But precisely because he is not absolutely good, no one among us can pose as an absolute judge and pronounce the definitive elimination of the worst among the guilty, because no one of us can lay claim to absolute innocence. Capital judgment upsets the only indisputable human solidarity – our solidarity against death – and it can be legitimized only by a truth or a principle that is superior to man.

In fact, the supreme punishment has always been, throughout the ages, a religious penalty. Inflicted in the name of the king, God's representative on earth, or by priests or in the name of society considered as a sacred body, it denies, not human solidarity, but the guilty man's membership in the divine community, the only thing that can give him life. Life on earth is taken from him, to be sure, but his chance of making amends is left him. The real judgment is not pronounced; it will be in the other world. Only religious values, and especially belief in eternal life, can therefore serve as a basis for the supreme punishment because, according to their own logic, they keep it from being definitive and irreparable. Consequently, it is justified only insofar as it is not supreme.

The Catholic Church, for example, has always accepted the necessity of the death penalty. It inflicted that penalty itself, and without stint, in other periods. Even today it justifies it and grants the State the right to apply it. The Church's position, however subtle, contains a very deep feeling that was expressed directly in 1937 by a Swiss National Councillor from Fribourg during a discussion in the National Council. According to M. Grand, the lowest of criminals when faced with execution withdraws into himself. 'He repents and his preparation for death is thereby facilitated. The Church has saved one of its members and fulfilled its divine mission. This is why it has always accepted the death penalty, not only as a means of self-defense, but *as a powerful means of salvation.** . . . Without trying to make of it a thing of the Church, the death penalty can point proudly to its almost divine efficacy, like war.'

By virtue of the same reasoning, probably, there could be read on the sword of the Fribourg executioner the words: 'Lord Jesus, thou art the judge.' Hence the executioner is invested with a sacred function. He is the man who destroys the body in order to deliver the soul to the divine sentence, which no one can judge beforehand. Some may think that such words imply rather

* My italics.

scandalous confusions. And, to be sure, whoever clings to the teaching of Jesus will look upon
that handsome sword as one more outrage to the
person of Christ. In the light of this, it is possible
to understand the dreadful remark of the Russian
condemned man about to be hanged by the Tsar's
executioners in 1905 who said firmly to the priest
who had come to console him with the image of
Christ: 'Go away and commit no sacrilege.' The
unbeliever cannot keep from thinking that men
who have set at the center of their faith the stag-
gering victim of a judicial error ought at least to
hesitate before committing legal murder. Believers might also be reminded that Emperor Julian,
before his conversion, did not want to give official
offices to Christians because they systematically
refused to pronounce death sentences or to have
anything to do with them. For five centuries
Christians therefore believed that the strict moral
teaching of their master forbade killing. But Catholic faith is not nourished solely by the personal
teaching of Christ. It also feeds on the Old Testament, on St Paul, and on the Church Fathers.
In particular, the immortality of the soul and the
universal resurrection of bodies are articles of
dogma. As a result, capital punishment is for the

believer a temporary penalty that leaves the final sentence in suspense, an arrangement necessary only for terrestrial order, an administrative measure which, far from signifying the end for the guilty man, may instead favor his redemption. I am not saying that all believers agree with this, and I can readily imagine that some Catholics may stand closer to Christ than to Moses or St Paul. I am simply saying that faith in the immortality of the soul allowed Catholicism to see the problem of capital punishment in very different terms and to justify it.

But what is the value of such a justification in the society we live in, which in its institutions and its customs has lost all contact with the sacred? When an atheistic or skeptical or agnostic judge inflicts the death penalty on an unbelieving criminal, he is pronouncing a definitive punishment that cannot be reconsidered. He takes his place on the throne of God,* without having the same powers and even without believing in God. He kills, in short, because his ancestors believed in eternal life. But the society that he claims to

* As everyone knows, the jury's decision is preceded by the words: 'Before God and my conscience . . .'

represent is in reality pronouncing a simple measure of elimination, doing violence to the human community united against death, and taking a stand as an absolute value because society is laying claim to absolute power. To be sure, it delegates a priest to the condemned man, through tradition. The priest may legitimately hope that fear of punishment will help the guilty man's conversion. Who can accept, however, that such a calculation should justify a penalty most often inflicted and received in a quite different spirit? It is one thing to believe before being afraid and another to find faith after fear. Conversion through fire or the guillotine will always be suspect, and it may seem surprising that the Church has not given up conquering infidels through terror. In any case, society that has lost all contact with the sacred can find no advantage in a conversion in which it professes to have no interest. Society decrees a sacred punishment and at the same time divests it both of excuse and of usefulness. Society proceeds sovereignly to eliminate the evil ones from her midst as if she were virtue itself. Like an honorable man killing his wayward son and remarking: 'Really, I didn't know what to do with him.' She assumes the right to select as if she were nature herself and to add great sufferings to the elimination as if she were a redeeming god.

To assert, in any case, that a man must be absolutely cut off from society because he is absolutely evil amounts to saying that society is absolutely good, and no one in his right mind will believe this today. Instead of believing this, people will more readily think the reverse. Our society has become so bad and so criminal only because she has respected nothing but her own preservation or a good reputation in history. Society has indeed lost all contact with the sacred. But society began in the nineteenth century to find a substitute for religion by proposing herself as an object of adoration. The doctrines of evolution and the notions of selection that accompany them have made of the future of society a final end. The political utopias that were grafted onto those doctrines placed at the end of time a golden age that justified in advance any enterprises whatever. Society became accustomed to legitimizing what might serve her future and, consequently, to making use of the supreme punishment in an absolute way. From then on, society considered as a crime and a sacrilege anything that stood in the way of her plan and her temporal dogmas. In other words, after being a priest, the executioner became a government official. The result is here all around us. The situation is such that this mid-century society which has lost the right, in all logics, to decree capital punishment ought now to suppress it for reasons of realism.

In relation to crime, how can our civilization be defined? The reply is easy: for thirty years now, State crimes have been far more numerous than individual crimes. I am not even speaking of wars, general or localized, although bloodshed too is an alcohol that eventually intoxicates like the headiest of wines. But the number of individuals killed directly by the State has assumed astronomical proportions and infinitely outnumbers private murders. There are fewer and fewer condemned by common law and more and more condemned for political reasons. The proof is that each of us, however honorable he may be, can foresee the possibility of being someday condemned to death, whereas that eventuality would have seemed ridiculous at the beginning of the century. Alphonse Karr's witty remark: 'Let the noble assassins begin' has no meaning now. Those who cause the most blood to flow are the same ones who believe they have right, logic, and history on their side.

Hence our society must now defend herself not so much against the individual as against the State. It may be that the proportions will be reversed in another thirty years. But, for the moment, our self-defense must be aimed at the State first and foremost. Justice and expediency command the law to protect the individual against a State given over to the follies of sectarianism or of pride. 'Let the State begin and abolish the death penalty' ought to be our rallying cry today.

Bloodthirsty laws, it has been said, make bloodthirsty customs. But any society eventually reaches a state of ignominy in which, despite every disorder, the customs never manage to be as bloodthirsty as the laws. Half of Europe knows that condition. We French knew it in the past and may again know it. Those executed during the Occupation led to those executed at the time of the Liberation, whose friends now dream of revenge. Elsewhere States laden with too many crimes are getting ready to drown their guilt in even greater massacres. One kills for a nation or a class that has been granted divine status. One kills for a future society that has likewise been given divine status.

Whoever thinks he has omniscience imagines he has omnipotence. Temporal idols demanding an absolute faith tirelessly decree absolute punishments. And religions devoid of transcendence kill great numbers of condemned men devoid of hope.

How can European society of the mid-century survive unless it decides to defend individuals by every means against the State's oppression? Forbidding a man's execution would amount to proclaiming publicly that society and the State are not absolute values, that nothing authorizes them to legislate definitively or to bring about the irreparable. Without the death penalty, Gabriel Péri and Brasillach would perhaps be among us. We could then judge them according to our opinion and proudly proclaim our judgment, whereas now they judge us and we keep silent. Without the death penalty Rajk's corpse would not poison Hungary; Germany, with less guilt on her conscience, would be more favorably looked upon by Europe; the Russian Revolution would not be agonizing in shame; and Algerian blood would weigh less heavily on our consciences. Without the death penalty, Europe would not be infected by the corpses accumulated for the last twenty years in its tired soil. On our continent, all values are upset by fear and hatred between individuals and between nations. In the conflict of ideas the weapons are the cord and the guillotine. A natural and human society exercising her right of repression has given way to a dominant ideology that requires human sacrifices. 'The example of the gallows,' it has been written, 'is that a man's life ceases to be sacred when it is thought useful to kill him.' Apparently it is becoming ever more useful; the example is being copied; the contagion is spreading everywhere. And together with it, the disorder of nihilism. Hence we must call a spectacular halt and proclaim, in our principles and institutions, that the individual is above the State. And any measure that decreases the pressure of social forces upon the individual will help to relieve the congestion of a Europe suffering from a rush of blood, allowing us to think more clearly and to start on the way toward health. Europe's malady consists in believing nothing and claiming to know everything. But Europe is far from knowing everything, and, judging from the revolt and hope we feel, she believes in something: she believes that the extreme of man's wretchedness, on some mysterious limit, borders on the extreme of his greatness. For the majority of Europeans, faith is lost. And with it, the justifications faith provided in the domain of punishment. But the majority of Europeans also reject the State idolatry that aimed to take the place of faith. Henceforth in mid-course, both certain and uncertain, having made up our minds never to submit and never to oppress, we should admit at one and the same time our hope and our ignorance, we should refuse absolute law and the irreparable judgment. We know enough to say that this or that major criminal deserves hard labor for life. But we don't know enough to decree that he be shorn of his future – in other words, of the chance we all have of making amends. Because of what I have just said, in the unified Europe of the future the solemn abolition of the death penalty ought to be the first article of the European Code we all hope for.

From the humanitarian idylls of the eighteenth century to the bloodstained gallows the way leads directly, and the executioners of today, as everyone knows, are humanists. Hence we cannot be too wary of the humanitarian ideology in dealing with a problem such as the death penalty. On the point of concluding, I should like therefore to repeat that neither an illusion as to the natural goodness of the human being nor faith in a golden age to come motivates my opposition to the death penalty. On the contrary, its abolition seems to me necessary because of reasoned pessimism, of logic, and of realism. Not that the heart has no share in what I have said. Anyone who has spent weeks with texts, recollections, and men having any contact, whether close or not, with the gallows could not possibly remain untouched by that experience. But, let me repeat, I do not believe, nonetheless, that there is no responsibility in this world and that we must give way to that modern tendency to absolve everything, victim and murderer, in the same confusion. Such purely sentimental confusion is made up of cowardice rather than of generosity and eventually justifies whatever is worst in this world. If you keep on excusing, you eventually give your blessing to the slave camp, to cowardly force, to organized executioners, to the cynicism of great political monsters; you finally hand over your brothers. This can be seen around us. But it so happens, in the present state of the world, that the man of today wants laws and institutions suitable to a convalescent, which will curb him without breaking him and lead him without crushing him. Hurled into the unchecked dynamic movement of history, he needs a natural philosophy and a few laws of equilibrium. He needs, in short, a society based on reason and not the anarchy into which he has been plunged by his own pride and the excessive powers of the State.

I am convinced that abolition of the death penalty would help us progress toward that society. After taking such an initiative, France could offer to extend it to the non-abolitionist countries on both sides of the iron curtain. But, in any case, she should set the example. Capital punishment would then be replaced by hard labor – for life in the case of criminals considered irremediable and for a fixed period in the case of the others. To any who feel that such a penalty is harsher than capital punishment we can only express our amazement that they did not suggest, in this case, reserving it for such as Landru and applying capital punishment to minor criminals. We might remind them, too, that hard labor leaves the condemned man the possibility of choosing death, whereas the guillotine offers no alternative. To any who feel, on the other hand, that hard labor is too mild a penalty, we can answer first that they lack imagination and secondly that privation of freedom seems to them a slight punishment only insofar as contemporary society has taught us to despise freedom.*

The fact that Cain is not killed but bears a mark of reprobation in the eyes of men is the lesson we must draw from the Old Testament, to say nothing of the Gospels, instead of looking back to the cruel examples of the Mosaic law. In any case, nothing keeps us from trying out an experiment, limited in duration (ten years, for instance), if our Parliament is still incapable of making up for its votes in favor of alcohol by such a great civilizing step as complete abolition of the penalty. And if, really, public opinion and its representatives

* See the report on the death penalty by Representative Dupont in the National Assembly on 31 May 1791: 'A sharp and burning mood consumes the assassin; the thing he fears most is inactivity; it leaves him to himself, and to get away from it he continually braves death and tries to cause death in others; solitude and his own conscience are his real torture. Does this not suggest to you what kind of punishment should be inflicted on him, what is the kind to which he will be most sensitive? *Is it not in the nature of the malady that the remedy is to be found?*' I have italicized the last sentence, for it makes of that little-known Representative a true precursor of our modern psychology.

cannot give up the law of laziness which simply
eliminates what it cannot reform, let us at least –
while hoping for a new day of truth – not make
of it the 'solemn slaughterhouse' that befouls our
society. The death penalty as it is now applied,
and however rarely it may be, is a revolting butch-
ery, an outrage inflicted on the person and body
of man. That truncation, that living and yet
uprooted head, those spurts of blood date from
a barbarous period that aimed to impress the
masses with degrading sights. Today when such
vile death is administered on the sly, what is the
meaning of this torture? The truth is that in the
nuclear age we kill as we did in the age of the
spring balance. And there is not a man of normal
sensitivity who, at the mere thought of such crude
surgery, does not feel nauseated. If the French
State is incapable of overcoming habit and giving
Europe one of the remedies it needs, let France
begin by reforming the manner of administering
capital punishment. The science that serves to kill
so many could at least serve to kill decently. An
anesthetic that would allow the condemned man
to slip from sleep to death (which would be left
within his reach for at least a day so that he could
use it freely and would be administered to him

in another form if he were unwilling or weak of will) would assure his elimination, if you insist, but would put a little decency into what is at present but a sordid and obscene exhibition.

I suggest such compromises only insofar as one must occasionally despair of seeing wisdom and true civilization influence those responsible for our future. For certain men, more numerous than we think, it is physically unbearable to know what the death penalty really is and not to be able to prevent its application. In their way, they suffer that penalty themselves, and without any justice. If only the weight of filthy images weighing upon them were reduced, society would lose nothing. But even that, in the long run, will be inadequate. There will be no lasting peace either in the heart of individuals or in social customs until death is outlawed.